DevOps & DevSecOps

Evolution of Approaches in IT

Fabrizio Zuccari

"DevOps e DevSecOps sono i pennelli con cui dipingiamo il quadro dell'innovazione tecnologica, unendo la creatività dello sviluppo all'integrità della sicurezza. La bellezza dei risultati dipende dalla maestria con cui li maneggiamo."

"DevOps and DevSecOps are the brushes with which we paint the canvas of technological innovation, blending the creativity of development with the integrity of security. The beauty of the results depends on the skill with which we wield them."

Table of Contents

DevOps 5

DevOps 1:Introduction to DevOps 6

    Definition of DevOps 6
    History and Origin of DevOps 7
    Benefits of DevOps 8
    DevOps vs. Traditional Development and Operations 9
DevOps 2: Automation and DevOps Tools 11

    Automation Principles 11
    Automation Tools 12
    Source Code Management and Versioning 14
    Continuous Integration (CI) e Continuous Delivery (CD) 15
DevOps 3: Collaboration and Communication 16

    Culture of Collaboration and Communication 16
    DevOps team and Roles (Dev, Ops, QA) 18
    Best Practices for Team Communication 19
    Collaboration Across the CI/CD Pipeline 21
DevOps 4: Infrastructure as Code (IaC) 23

    What is IaC 24
    Advantages of IaC 24
    IaC Tools 25
    Practical Examples of Infrastructure as Code
    Management 27
DevOps 5: Monitoring and Log Management 29

    Application and Infrastructure Monitoring 29
    Log Management and Data Analysis 31
    Tools for Monitoring and Log Management 33
    Troubleshooting and Performance Improvements 34
DevSecOps 37

DevSecOps 1: Introduction to DevSecOps 38

    Definition of DevSecOps: 38
    The Role of Security in a DevOps Environment 39
    Representation of a DevSecOps Implementation 40

Risks Associated with the Lack of Security in a DevOps Environment 42

DevSecOps 2: Integration of Security into DevOps Processes 43

DevSecOps Model 44
Tools for Security Integration 45
Vulnerability Management Practices 47
DevSecOps 3: Application Security 48

Common Application Vulnerabilities: 48
Secure Development Practices: 50
Source code control 52
Automation of Application Security Testing 53
DevSecOps 4: Security of Infrastructure and Orchestration
....56

Security of Infrastructure as Code 56
Containers and Orchestration 59
Access Control and Authentication 60
Network and Data Security 62
DevSecOps 5: Security Incident Management 65

Detection of Security Incidents 65
Incident Planning and Response (CSIRT) 67
Digital Forensic Analysis 68
Post Incident Improvements 70
DevSecOps 6: Compliance and Security Regulations 72

Key Security Regulations 73
Security and Compliance Audits 75
Compliance Automation 77
Security Governance 79

DevOps

DevOps 1:Introduction to DevOps

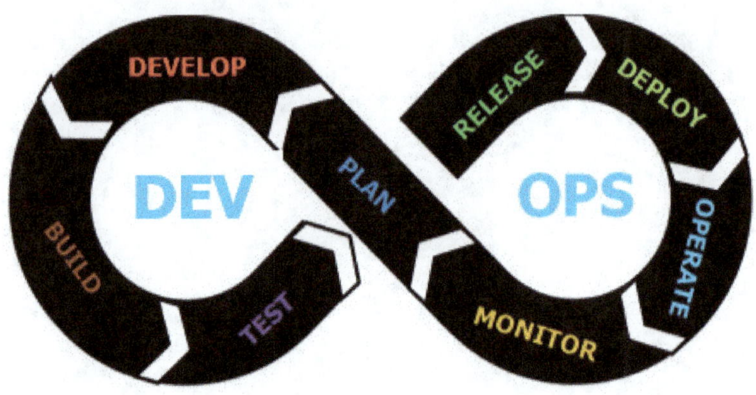

In the increasingly competitive and dynamic landscape of the software industry, companies are constantly seeking ways to enhance the efficiency and agility of their development and operations processes.

It is in this context that DevOps, an innovative and transformative approach, has emerged as a response to the challenges posed by the need to deliver high-quality software quickly and reliably.

Definition of DevOps

DevOps is a philosophy, a methodology, and a set of practices aimed at improving collaboration between development (Dev) and operations (Ops) teams within an organization. The term "DevOps" is a combination of "Development" and "Operations," and its primary goal is to break down the barriers between these traditionally separate functions, promoting a culture of collaboration, automation, shared responsibilities, and performance measurement.

Within the context of DevOps, development and operations activities are integrated synergistically to provide a continuous and seamless workflow, with shorter development cycles, more frequent releases, and a greater focus on software quality.

This means that DevOps professionals work together to automate processes, continuously test software, release reliably, and manage infrastructure more efficiently.

History and Origin of DevOps

The history of DevOps traces its roots back to the early 2000s, a pivotal period when businesses began to recognize the limitations imposed by traditional divisions between development and operations departments. This rigid separation posed significant obstacles to the software development and release process, substantially slowing down the entire production cycle.

It's essential to note that the growth of the Agile culture and the adoption of methodologies like Scrum laid the foundation for increased collaboration between development and operations teams during this time. These new methodologies promoted a more flexible and collaboration-oriented approach, contrasting with the rigidity of traditional divisions.

However, the term "DevOps" received a distinctive name and a clear definition only in 2009, thanks to the contribution of Patrick Debois, one of the pioneering visionaries of this movement. This moment marked a turning point in the history of DevOps because it allowed for a precise definition of the principles and practices that characterize it.

From that point onward, the DevOps movement gained rapid momentum, spreading worldwide. The speed with which it was adopted attests to the urgency of overcoming the divisions between development and operations and embracing a unified approach to software engineering. Organizations recognized the potential for radically improving the efficiency, quality, and speed of software development and management through DevOps. This approach enables companies to respond more quickly and effectively to customer needs and market changes while ensuring a high level of quality.

Today, DevOps is a common and indispensable practice in many organizations worldwide, bearing witness to the evolution and revolution that the software engineering sector has undergone in recent decades.

Benefits of DevOps

The adoption of DevOps brings several significant benefits to organizations that embrace it.

Some of these benefits include:

- **Faster and more frequent releases:**
  With DevOps, it is possible to automate much of the development, testing, and release process, allowing companies to release high-quality software more quickly and frequently. This is crucial for responding promptly to customer needs and market changes.

- **Improved software quality:**
  Automation of testing and release operations helps reduce human errors and improve software quality, resulting in fewer bugs and greater system stability.

- **Enhanced team collaboration:**
  DevOps promotes collaboration between developers

and system administrators, helping to eliminate barriers between these functions. This leads to a smoother workflow and better mutual understanding.

- **Greater operational efficiency:**
  Automation of operational processes reduces downtime and allows organizations to use resources more efficiently, resulting in reduced operational costs.

- **Increased agility and adaptability:**
  DevOps provides organizations with the flexibility needed to quickly adapt to market changes and customer demands, enabling greater business agility.

DevOps vs. Traditional Development and Operations

To fully grasp the value of DevOps, it's essential to compare it with traditional development and operations practices.

In the traditional approach, development and operations are often *siloed*, which can lead to a range of issues, including:

- **Infrequent and risky releases:**
  Releases are complex and risky events that require intensive planning. This slows down time to market and increases the risk of errors.

- **Poor communication:**
  Lack of communication between development and operations teams can lead to misunderstandings and

reduced effectiveness in problem-solving.

- **Manual processes:**
  Manual processes are susceptible to human errors
  and are time-consuming. This can result in additional
  delays and added costs.

DevOps, on the other hand, aims to overcome these
challenges by promoting collaboration, automation, and
shared responsibilities between development and
operations. This leads to greater efficiency, more frequent
releases, and improved software quality.

DevOps 2: Automation and DevOps Tools

Automation is a key element that enhances the efficiency, consistency, and quality of the entire development and operations process.

Automation Principles

- **Automation of repetitive tasks:**
  The DevOps mantra is clear: *automate everything that can be automated*. This includes tasks that are repetitive, tedious, and, most importantly, prone to errors. Within the DevOps domain, automation extends to a wide range of tasks, including:

  - Server installation and configuration,

  - Software releases,

  - system testing and monitoring.

By automating these processes, organizations eliminate human errors, save valuable time, and reduce the risk of disruptions.

- **Automation of the software lifecycle:**
Automation doesn't stop at the development or software release cycle. In a DevOps perspective, the entire software lifecycle is subject to automation. This means that from code writing to distribution and monitoring in production, each step is integrated into an automated and consistent workflow, resulting in regular and reliable releases with consistent software quality.

- **Infrastructure as Code (IaC):**
Another fundamental pillar of DevOps is the concept of managing infrastructure as code. In this approach, not only is software defined through code, but infrastructure itself is described through code. This means that servers, networks, databases, and other infrastructure resources are defined through code rather than being manually configured. This practice simplifies infrastructure management, automation, and orchestration, enabling rapid and consistent provisioning.
When needed, the infrastructure can be replicated or modified reliably, ensuring that the configuration always aligns with the application's requirements.

Automation Tools

Automation in DevOps is supported by a wide range of tools.
These tools serve to automate key activities in the development and operations cycle, offering a flexible and customizable way to implement automation principles.

Some of the major DevOps tools include:

- **Jenkins:**
  An automation tool for building and releasing software, allowing the creation of custom CI/CD (Continuous Integration/Continuous Delivery) pipelines.

- **Ansible:**
  An infrastructure automation system that efficiently manages server configuration and distribution.

- **Docker:**
  A containerization platform that simplifies application deployment in isolated environments, ensuring consistency between development and production.

- **Kubernetes:**
  A container orchestration system that streamlines application management and load balancing in containerized environments.

- **Terraform:**
  A tool for defining and managing infrastructure as code, facilitating automated infrastructure creation and maintenance.

- **Chef e Puppet:**
  Configuration automation tools that enable the definition and consistent application of configurations to servers and infrastructure resources.

These are just some examples of the many tools available for implementing automation in a DevOps context.

The choice of tools depends on the specific needs of the organization and the project, but they all share the goal of simplifying and improving the development and operations processes through automation.

Source Code Management and Versioning

Source code management and versioning are critical aspects that enable efficient collaboration and the maintenance of a precise record of changes made to the software.

In this context, Git takes center stage as a fundamental tool.

Git:

Git is a distributed version control system that has established itself as the preferred solution for developers and organizations worldwide. Its significance lies in its ability to track and manage changes to the source code efficiently and collaboratively.

One of Git's distinctive features is its distributed nature. Each developer has a complete copy of the repository they work on, which allows for unprecedented flexibility and freedom. Developers can work offline and synchronize their changes with the main repository when they are ready. This promotes seamless collaboration and accurate versioning.

Every time a change is made to the source code, Git meticulously tracks it. This allows you to trace back to any previous version of the software and compare changes quickly and efficiently.

The use of Git is essential for maintaining a complete history of changes made to the software, which is crucial for issue resolution and rolling back to previous versions in case of errors or emergency situations. This ability to "time travel" with your code provides greater peace of mind when making changes and releases.

Continuous Integration (CI) e Continuous Delivery (CD)

Continuous Integration (CI) and Continuous Delivery (CD) re two closely related DevOps practices aimed at ensuring a smooth and reliable development and distribution workflow.

Continuous Integration (CI):
CI is a fundamental pillar of DevOps that involves the automatic integration of code changes into the main repository multiple times a day. Developers consistently submit their code to a CI system that runs automated tests to verify its functionality and compatibility with existing software. This practice promptly identifies errors or conflicts, allowing developers to resolve them quickly and keep the code operational. CI promotes code quality, consistency, and stability.

Continuous Delivery (CD):
CD is a natural extension of CI, as it goes beyond integration and involves software release.
Software that successfully passes CI tests is automatically released into a production or pre-production environment. This process enables fast and reliable releases, minimizing the risk of human errors and significantly simplifying software deployment.

DevOps 3: Collaboration and Communication

Within the DevOps ecosystem, collaboration and communication play a crucial role, acting as the glue that binds development (Dev), operations (Ops), and quality assurance (QA) teams together.

Let's explore best practices for effective communication among teams:

Culture of Collaboration and Communication

A culture of collaboration and communication is the beating heart of DevOps, as it is what creates the fertile ground for synergy among the various players involved in software development, release, and management.

This culture is built on key principles that guide the action and mindset of DevOps teams:

- **Transparency:**
Transparency is the foundation upon which all other collaboration practices are built. In a DevOps culture, every team member has access to relevant information, data, and processes. This ensures that everyone has a clear view of the big picture, enabling them to make informed decisions and avoid misunderstandings. Information sharing is at the core of open communication and the ability to collaboratively solve problems.

- **Shared Responsibility:**
In DevOps, the success of the entire software lifecycle is a shared responsibility among Dev, Ops, and QA teams. No team operates in isolation, and each has a significant role in delivering high-quality software. This approach eliminates barriers between teams and promotes continuous collaboration. Shared responsibilities foster a sense of collective ownership for the end result, encouraging everyone to work together for success.

- **Continuous Learning:**
The DevOps culture embraces continuous learning as a central value. This implies an open mindset towards change and innovation. Mistakes are seen as learning opportunities, and improvements are constantly incorporated. This adaptation-oriented mindset helps keep DevOps teams flexible, capable of effectively responding to the evolving needs of the market and the organization itself.

DevOps team and Roles (Dev, Ops, QA)

Within a DevOps team, there are several key roles:

- **Developers (Dev):**
  Developers are the beating heart of the DevOps team. They are the code creators, application designers, and agents of continuous improvement. Their work focuses on writing high-quality code, designing features, and optimizing performance. They collaborate closely with other DevOps team members, ensuring that the code meets quality standards and is ready for release.

- **System Administrators and Operations (Ops):**
  System administrators and operations are the custodians of the infrastructure that supports the applications. Their primary responsibility is to ensure that applications run reliably and efficiently. They automate operational processes, manage resources, monitor performance, and promptly respond to any issues. Through automation and proactive management, they reduce downtime and enable fast and stable releases.

- **Quality Assurance (QA):**
  The quality assurance team plays a critical role in ensuring that the software meets quality requirements. They are responsible for software verification and validation through rigorous testing. By conducting functional, performance, and security tests, they ensure that the software is free from bugs and compliant with quality specifications. Any issues or discrepancies found are reported to developers and operators for immediate correction.

- **Additional Roles:**
  In addition to the key roles mentioned above, some organizations have other essential roles:

  - **Security Team:**
    These specialists focus on the security of software and infrastructure. They collaborate with developers, system administrators, and the quality assurance team to identify and address vulnerabilities and threats. Security is a growing concern in the DevOps world, and these professionals play a crucial role in ensuring that software is protected from potential risks.

  - **Release Managers:**
    These professionals are responsible for planning and coordinating software releases. They manage the preparation and release phases, ensuring that software is distributed effectively and reliably. They work closely with developers, system administrators, and the quality assurance team to ensure error-free releases.

Best Practices for Team Communication

Effective communication is a fundamental pillar in the DevOps approach as it fosters collaboration and synergy among Dev, Ops, and QA teams.

To ensure that communication is efficient and productive, it's important to follow some key best practices:

- **Regular Meetings:**
  Organizing regular meetings among Dev, Ops, and QA teams is essential to keep everyone on the same

page. These meetings should be well-planned and structured to be effective. During these sessions, teams can discuss project status, emerging issues, and possible solutions. This approach allows all team members to stay informed and collaborate to achieve common goals.

- **Collaboration Tools:**
  The use of collaboration tools is crucial in facilitating communication and efficiently resolving issues. Chat platforms, ticketing systems, and project management software are tools that help DevOps teams share information and collaborate in real-time. These tools streamline communication, allowing teams to stay updated on project status and respond quickly to challenges that may arise.

- **Knowledge sharing:**
  Knowledge sharing is a key element of effective communication among teams. Developers can explain how the application works and share information about the code, while system administrators can describe how the underlying infrastructure is configured. This knowledge sharing creates mutual understanding and helps teams make informed decisions and solve problems collaboratively.

- **Process Automation:**
  Automating communication processes is an important step in reducing the potential for human errors and ensuring greater efficiency. For example, automation can be used to report errors or request resources. This allows teams to focus on high-value tasks, minimizing repetitive and redundant activities.

Collaboration Across the CI/CD Pipeline

Collaboration among Dev, Ops, and QA teams extends seamlessly through the Continuous Integration (CI) and Continuous Delivery (CD) pipeline. Within this pipeline, teams collaborate to automate the workflow from code development to software release, fostering a culture of continuous improvement and synergy.

In the CI phase, developers consistently integrate code into the shared repository while triggering automated tests. Collaboration is inherent in the design of these tests, bug identification, and issue resolution, with teams working collectively to ensure that the code is not only functional but also of high quality. This iterative process encourages feedback loops that lead to improvements, thus enhancing the overall product.

As we move to the CD phase, system administrators take charge of automating the release and deployment processes, while the quality control team rigorously verifies the software's quality before release. This cross-team collaboration ensures that the software is primed for production, facilitating swift and reliable releases.

Several best practices, including regular meetings, collaboration tools, knowledge sharing, and process automation, form the backbone of this collaborative culture. Regular meetings ensure that everyone is aligned and informed, allowing for real-time issue resolution. Collaboration tools enable efficient communication and problem-solving, ensuring that the entire team is on the same page. Knowledge sharing helps bridge the gap

between different skill sets and expertise, promoting a deeper understanding of the system.
Furthermore, process automation streamlines routine tasks, reducing human error, and allowing teams to focus on more value-added activities. This comprehensive approach not only enhances collaboration but also fosters a culture of continuous learning and adaptation, ultimately leading to more effective and efficient DevOps practices.

DevOps 4: Infrastructure as Code (IaC)

Infrastructure as Code (IaC) is another pillar of DevOps that allows you to manage IT infrastructure in a manner like how you manage the source code of applications.

This methodology offers numerous advantages, including consistency, scalability, versioning, and automation. IaC tools such as **Terraform**, **CloudFormation**, and **Ansible** simplify the implementation of this methodology, enabling DevOps teams to manage infrastructure efficiently and consistently.

What is IaC

IaC represents a revolutionary approach to managing IT infrastructure.

It allows DevOps teams to define the entire infrastructure, including servers, networks, databases, and other resources, using programming languages or configuration files. In other words, instead of manually configuring each component of the infrastructure, you can create scripts or declarative definitions that describe the desired state. These definitions can be treated as code, versioned, controlled through source code management systems like Git, and integrated into the CI/CD pipeline. The goal is to automate the provisioning, configuration, and management of these resources in a consistent and repeatable manner.

A concrete example of IaC could be a configuration file that defines the creation of a web server, specifying the operating system, applications to install, and firewall rules to apply. This configuration file can then be executed through an IaC tool to automatically create the server without direct human intervention.

Advantages of IaC

The adoption of IaC brings several significant advantages: it allows teams to automate the provisioning and configuration of resources, improve consistency and scalability, facilitate versioning, and promote collaboration among teams.

- **Consistency:**
  Infrastructure managed through IaC is highly consistent because the definitions are repeatable and uniform. This reduces the risk of human errors and simplifies maintenance.

- **Scalability:**
  In a cloud or data center environment, infrastructure can be scaled efficiently. Using IaC definitions, configuration patterns can be easily replicated, allowing for dynamic resource growth when needed.

- **Versioning:**
  Thanks to the use of source code control tools, IaC definitions can be versioned. This means that you can keep track of changes, making it easier to roll back to a previous configuration in case of issues or collaborate among team members.

- **Automation:**
  Automation is at the core of IaC. This enables the automation of resource provisioning and management, reducing the time required to implement and manage infrastructure.

- **Collaboration:**
  Since IaC definitions are code, they promote greater collaboration between Dev and Ops teams. This fosters a shared understanding of the infrastructure and requirements, allowing for a smoother and shared workflow across different functions.

IaC Tools

As mentioned earlier, there are tools for IaC that simplify the implementation of this methodology:

- **Terraform:**

  Terraform is an open-source tool developed by HashiCorp. It allows you to define, configure, and manage infrastructure as code. Terraform is known for its support for a wide range of cloud providers, making it flexible and suitable for heterogeneous environments. With Terraform, teams can write code that describes the desired resources (such as servers, networks, databases, firewalls, etc.), specifying the properties of these resources. Terraform then takes care of provisioning and configuring these resources, ensuring they are consistent with the code definition.

A practical example of using Terraform could be creating a server on a cloud platform. By defining the server's specifications and associated resources, such as networks and disks, teams can write Terraform code that automates the creation of the server and its resources. If needed, this code can be easily updated or modified to adapt to new requirements.

- **AWS CloudFormation:**

AWS CloudFormation is a tool specifically designed for the Amazon Web Services (AWS) environment that allows you to define AWS resources using JSON or YAML templates and manage them as code. This tool is particularly useful for those operating in an AWS environment.

It enables DevOps teams to define the entire AWS infrastructure, including EC2 instances, RDS databases, auto-scaling stacks, VPC networks, and more, using a declarative language. The infrastructure can be created, updated, and even deleted as part of an automated workflow.

Ansible:

Ansible is a configuration automation tool that can be used to implement Infrastructure as Code (IaC). While it's not a pure IaC tool, Ansible is extremely useful for defining server configurations and automating resource provisioning and management. Ansible uses modules and playbooks, written in YAML, to define how resources should be configured. With Ansible, teams can ensure server configurations are consistent and can automate complex tasks like software installation, service configuration, and more.

Practical Examples of Infrastructure as Code Management

The practical examples below demonstrate how Infrastructure as Code (IaC) can be successfully applied in various contexts to automate infrastructure provisioning, configuration, and management.

- **Provisioning a Server:**
  Let's say a team needs to create a new web server. Using Terraform, they can write code that defines the server, specifying details such as the operating system, compute resources, networks, firewall rules, and more. This Terraform code can then be executed to create the server in a cloud or on-

premises environment. In the future, if server specifications change or a new one is needed, simply make changes to the Terraform code and rerun it.

- **Configuring a Container Cluster:**
  In the world of containers, infrastructure management is highly dynamic. Using Kubernetes and YAML configuration files, you can define a container cluster. These YAML files specify container images, the number of replicas, load balancing rules, environment variables, and other configurations. This cluster can be created, updated, and managed as code. With a declarative definition, you can easily modify container configurations and deploy them across a cluster without manually performing complex operations on each host.

- **Implementing Security Policies:**
  To ensure the security of resources, such as servers or networks, you can use Ansible or similar tools. Through Ansible, you can define security policies, such as firewall rules or system security configurations. These definitions are written as Ansible code and can be automatically applied to different servers or networks, ensuring consistency in configuration and enhancing overall system security.

DevOps 5: Monitoring and Log Management

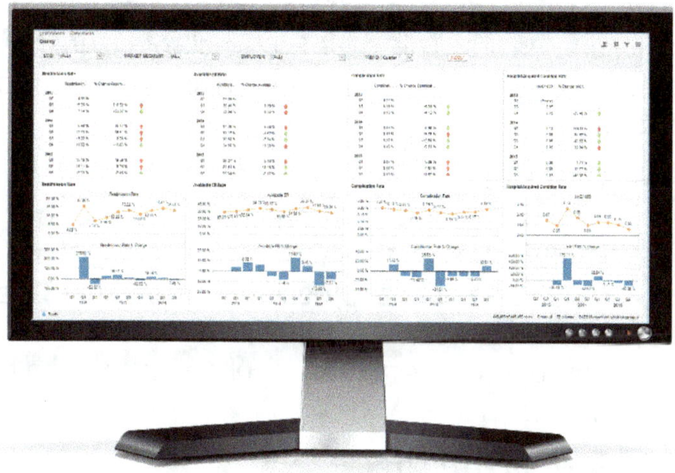

Monitoring and log management are essential components that enable proactive issue detection, event tracking, performance enhancement, and the assurance of application and infrastructure reliability.

The use of tools like **Prometheus**, **ELK Stack**, and **Splunk** simplifies data collection and analysis, enabling DevOps teams to make informed decisions and swiftly resolve issues.

Application and Infrastructure Monitoring

Monitoring is the process of real-time detection and recording of the performance and status of applications and infrastructure. This process allows for the proactive identification of anomalies, errors, or issues, enabling their resolution before they can adversely impact end users. Key aspects of monitoring include:

- **Application Monitoring:**
  Application monitoring focuses on the detection and recording of key metrics related to application performance. These metrics may include CPU usage, memory utilization, request response times, and application errors. This data is crucial to ensure the proper functioning of applications and their resource efficiency.

  - **CPU Usage:**
    By monitoring CPU usage, it is possible to identify moments when an application may require additional processing resources. This can indicate an issue or the need to appropriately scale the application to handle the workload.

  - **Memory Usage:**
    Monitoring memory usage allows for the assessment of resource utilization efficiency and the identification of potential memory leaks or memory management issues.

  - **Request Response Times:**
    Monitoring request response times helps verify whether applications are responding promptly. Slow response times can be a sign of performance issues.

  - **Application Errors:**
    Monitoring application errors helps detect bugs or functional problems. Errors can be detected, enabling timely intervention and resolution.

- **Infrastructure Monitoring:**
  Infrastructure monitoring involves the detection of the state of fundamental infrastructure components,

including servers, networks, virtual machines, and other elements. This process is essential for identifying system-level issues and addressing them before they impact applications running on this infrastructure:

- **Server**:
  Server monitoring allows verification of the operational status of servers, including resource utilization, network connectivity, and the integrity of the operating system.

- **Network**:
  Network monitoring is crucial for identifying congestion, network interruptions, or fluctuations in network performance. This helps prevent service disruptions and connectivity issues

- **Virtual Machines**:
  In virtualized or cloud environments, monitoring of virtual machines is essential to ensure that virtual instances are functioning correctly and have the required resources.

- **Other Infrastructure Components**:
  Infrastructure monitoring may also include components like databases, storage devices, and other critical services.

Log Management and Data Analysis

Logs, understood as detailed records of application and system activities, play a crucial role in the DevOps approach. Log management encompasses various stages, including log collection, storage, searching, and log analysis. This process is essential for issue identification, event tracking, performance enhancement, and ensuring the reliability of applications and infrastructure.

Below, we will delve into the key aspects of log management in more detail:

- **Collection:**
  Log collection is the first step in log management. Logs are generated by applications, servers, network devices, and other infrastructure components. These logs can contain a wide range of information, such as HTTP requests, system errors, user access, security events, and much more. Efficiently collecting these logs is crucial to have a comprehensive view of activities and events within the DevOps environment.

- **Storage:**
  Once collected, logs need to be securely and accessibly stored. This storage is essential for analysis, long-term monitoring, and regulatory compliance. In many cases, organizations are legally required to retain logs for a specific period. It is important to have a scalable and well-structured storage system that allows rapid access to log data when needed.

- **Analysis:**
  Log analysis is the heart of log management. It enables the identification of trends, recurring errors, and anomalous behaviors within the DevOps environment.
  Some key aspects of log analysis include:

  - **Problem Identification:**
    Log analysis helps pinpoint the root cause of issues. For example, logs can be used to trace the source of an exception in the code or examine an application's behavior prior to an abnormal termination. This process enables

the timely and accurate resolution of problems.

- **Performance Enhancement:** Monitoring data analysis can reveal opportunities to improve application and infrastructure performance. For instance, by identifying usage spikes or underutilized resources, it is possible to optimize resources and enhance the overall efficiency of the DevOps environment.

Tools for Monitoring and Log Management

There are numerous tools for monitoring and log management, among them there are:

- **Prometheus:**

Prometheus is a widely used open-source tool for monitoring applications and infrastructure.
This tool can collect monitoring data from various sources and provides a wide range of features for data analysis and visualization.

- **ELK Stack:**

The ELK Stack, composed of **E**lasticsearch, **L**ogstash

and **K**ibana is a suite of tools for log management. Elasticsearch serves as the log search and analysis engine, Logstash handles log ingestion, and Kibana provides a platform for data visualization.

- **Splunk:**

Splunk is a data analysis software that allows you to collect, store, search, and analyze logs and monitoring data from various sources. It is known for its real-time data analysis capabilities.

Troubleshooting and Performance Improvements

Troubleshooting and performance improvement are two primary goals, and monitoring and log management are the most appropriate tools to efficiently achieve them.

Let's see how these aspects can be leveraged to optimize the DevOps environment:

Troubleshooting:
Monitoring data and logs play a critical role in troubleshooting. The ability to identify the root cause of an issue is essential to ensure that applications and systems function reliably.
Here's how these tools can be used in this phase:

- **Cause Identification:**
  When an issue occurs, such as an application ceasing to function or a service slowing down, logs can be investigated to identify the cause of the problem. Detailed records can be examined to pinpoint errors or anomalous

behavior.

- **Event Tracking:**
  Logs provide a chronological trail of events, enabling operators to piece together a puzzle when an error occurs. This is particularly useful in understanding the sequence of events that led to a malfunction or abnormal termination.

- **Error Diagnosis:**
  When an application generates an exception, logs provide crucial information for understanding the cause of the error. This can significantly expedite the resolution process, allowing developers to intervene promptly.

- **Solution Verification:**
  After making corrections or changes, monitoring and log analysis help verify whether the implemented solutions have had the desired effect. This ensures that the problem has been effectively resolved.

- **Performance Improvements:**
  Performance improvement is a constant goal in DevOps because applications and infrastructure must operate efficiently. Monitoring data and log analysis play a key role in achieving this goal.
  Here's how they can be used to optimize performance:

  - **Peak Usage Detection:**
    By constantly monitoring key metrics, such as CPU usage, memory, and network traffic, you can detect peak usage. This allows for allocating additional resources when needed to prevent slowdowns or abnormal terminations.

- **Underutilized Resources:**
  On the other hand, log analysis can reveal underutilized resources. This indicates potential resource and cost wastage. By identifying and redistributing such resources more efficiently, you can optimize the DevOps environment.

- **Bottleneck Identification:**
  Logs can help identify critical points in the flow of applications and infrastructure. By detecting any blocks or delays, you can intervene to improve performance at those specific points.

- **Code Optimization:**
  Log analysis can also reveal inefficiencies in application code. By pinpointing areas of code that require improvements, developers can optimize application performance.

DevSecOps

DevSecOps 1: Introduction to DevSecOps

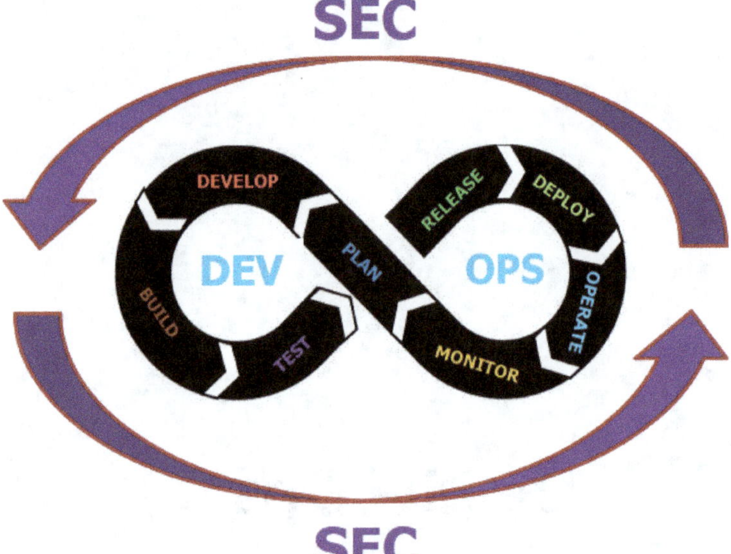

In the continuous evolution of DevOps, there has been a growing awareness of the importance of integrating security throughout the entire software development and IT operations lifecycle.

This has led to the emergence of DevSecOps: an approach that places security at the center of the entire DevOps process.

Definition of DevSecOps:

DevSecOps is a natural evolution of DevOps that emphasizes the integration of security at every phase of the software development and IT operations cycle. In contrast to the traditional approach where security is often a separate and delayed activity, DevSecOps promotes a culture in which security is the responsibility of every team member, from developers to system administrators. This means that security is not just a requirement but a fundamental element of design and implementation.

DevSecOps involves:

- **Collaboration:**
  Close collaboration between Dev (development) teams, Ops (operations management), and the security team is essential. Each of these teams must work together to ensure that security is integrated from the outset, from application design through development, release, and operations.

- **Security Automation:** Automation is a key pillar of DevSecOps. Automating security testing, source code scanning for vulnerabilities, identity and access management (IAM), and other security activities helps ensure the consistency and timeliness of security measures.

- **Continuous Risk Assessment:** Security is not static; therefore, DevSecOps promotes continuous risk assessment. This involves the ability to proactively identify, assess, and mitigate risks, as well as constantly monitoring the environment to detect potential threats.

The Role of Security in a DevOps Environment

Security plays a critical role in a DevOps environment for several reasons:

- **Protecting Sensitive Data:**
  In the digital world, safeguarding sensitive data is of paramount importance. Insecure applications or

infrastructures can become vulnerable to cyberattacks, jeopardizing sensitive data, corporate information, and user privacy.

- **Risk Reduction:** Integrating security throughout the development cycle helps proactively identify and mitigate risks. This contributes to preventing costly security incidents and damage to the company's reputation.

- **Regulatory Compliance:** Many industries are subject to specific regulations and standards that require data security and protection. DevSecOps helps ensure regulatory compliance by integrating security practices into processes.

Representation of a DevSecOps Implementation

A successful DevSecOps implementation can be represented as a continuous process where security is at the core of each phase. This approach ensures that security is integrated from the beginning and not overlooked.

- **Planning:**
  - The initial phase involves planning development activities, including identifying security requirements.
  - This is an opportunity for the team to assess potential project-related risks and define necessary security measures.

- **Secure Development:**
  - During the development phase, secure development practices are rigorously applied.
  - Static and dynamic code analysis is used to detect vulnerabilities and potential security

issues. This process helps ensure that the source code is robust and secure.

- **Testing and Validation:**
  - Code undergoes security testing, including penetration testing and vulnerability checks.
  - This phase is critical for identifying and resolving any vulnerabilities that may remain in the code, ensuring the application's resistance to attacks.

- **Secure Deployment:**
  - Continuous integration/continuous deployment (CI/CD) ensures that the source code is always ready for release, with all security checks applied.
  - This means that every iteration of the software undergoes security assessment and validation.

- **Continuous Monitoring:**
  - After deployment, systems are continuously monitored to detect real-time anomalies and threats.
  - The goal is to identify and respond quickly to potential breaches or security threats.

- **Incident Response:**
  - In the event of a breach or threat, incident response plans are defined.
  - These plans provide guidance on how to act swiftly to mitigate damage and restore system security.

Risks Associated with the Lack of Security in a DevOps Environment

The lack of security in a DevOps environment poses significant risks, including:

- **Data Vulnerabilities:**
  Without integrated security, sensitive data can be exposed to threats such as theft or breaches. This can lead to severe legal consequences and damage to the company's reputation.

- **Downtime and Service Loss:** Cyberattacks can cause downtime and service loss, resulting in financial losses and reputational damage.

- **Compromised Privacy:** Inadequate security can lead to the compromise of user privacy, with serious legal and ethical consequences.

- **Poor Regulatory Compliance:** Lack of regulatory compliance can lead to significant sanctions and fines. Companies must adhere to specific regulations related to data protection, privacy, and information security.

DevSecOps 2: Integration of Security into DevOps Processes

The DevSecOps approach represents a step forward from DevOps, emphasizing the importance of integrating security into every phase of the software development and operational lifecycle.

The use of specialized tools for code analysis, container scanning, and application testing helps effectively detect and mitigate vulnerabilities. Automating security tests during the CI/CD process ensures that applications are release-ready with the highest possible security, reducing risks and protecting sensitive data.

DevSecOps Model

In this model, security is not a separate activity or the sole responsibility of the security team but is shared by all DevOps team members.

Security is integrated at every step, ensuring that applications and infrastructure are robust and resilient against cyber threats. The goal is to reduce risks, protect sensitive data, and ensure regulatory compliance.

The following are the main phases of the DevSecOps model:

- **Secure Planning and Design:**
  In the initial phase, DevOps teams collaborate with the security team to identify and define security requirements for the application or infrastructure under development.
  This should also include assessing potential risks and defining security measures.

- **Secure Development:** During the development phase, best practices for secure development are rigorously applied.
  Also static and dynamic code analysis should be considered to identify and address potential vulnerabilities. It's the time to ensure that the source code is robust and secure from the start.

- **Security Testing and Validation:** In this phase, source code and applications undergo a series of automated and manual security tests.
  This include: penetration testing, vulnerability testing, and security reviews. The goal is to identify and address vulnerabilities before release.

- **Secure Deployment:** Continuous deployment (CI/CD) ensures that the source code is deployment-ready with all security controls applied. The CI/CD pipeline also includes automated security checks, such as container vulnerability scanning and code library checks.

- **Continuous Monitoring:** After deployment, systems are continuously monitored to detect real-time anomalies, threats, or breaches. The goal is to quickly identify potential threats and respond promptly.

- **Incident Response:** In the event of a breach or threat, incident response plans are ready to be executed to mitigate damage and restore security. This phase also includes post-incident analysis to improve future preparedness.

Tools for Security Integration

Integrating security into DevSecOps requires the use of specialized tools that support the detection, analysis, and mitigation of vulnerabilities. These tools are essential to ensure that applications and infrastructure are robust and resilient against cyber threats.

Below, we'll discuss some of the key tools used in a DevSecOps environment:

- **Static Application Security Testing (SAST):** Tools such as *Checkmarx* and *Fortify* perform static analysis of the source code to identify security vulnerabilities during the development process. These tools examine the code without running it and detect potential security issues such as known vulnerabilities, logical weaknesses, and programming errors.

- **Dynamic Application Security Testing (DAST):** Tools like *OWASP ZAP* and *Nessus* conduct runtime security testing to identify application-level vulnerabilities. These tools simulate attacks and analyze the application's behavior during execution to detect potential weaknesses.

- **Container Security Scanning:** With the widespread adoption of Docker containers, tools like *Clair* and *Anchore* become essential.
  They scan Docker containers to identify known vulnerabilities in container components, ensuring that container images are secure.

- **Vulnerability Management:** Platforms like *Veracode* and *WhiteSource* provide vulnerability management capabilities.
  These tools allow for the identification, classification, and planning of fixes for detected vulnerabilities. They also help track the status of fixes and ensure timely implementation.

- **Web Vulnerability Scanners:**
  For web applications, tools like *Burp Suite* and *Qualys Web Application Scanning* conduct automated security testing.
  These scanners identify common vulnerabilities, such as OWASP vulnerabilities, and help protect web applications from common attacks like SQL injection and cross-site scripting (XSS).

- **API Security Testing:** APIs (**A**pplication **P**rogramming **I**nterfaces) serve as the glue between various application components. API security testing is crucial to ensure secure communications between these components and protect against potential attacks.
  Testing tools like *Postman* and *OWASP API Security* allow for specific API testing.

- **Container Scanning:** Containers, often used in application deployment, must be secure. Before release, Docker containers are scanned to identify vulnerabilities in the images. Tools like Clair and Anchore perform these scans and provide detailed reports on detected vulnerabilities.

Vulnerability Management Practices

Vulnerability management is a critical aspect of DevSecOps and involves practices that help ensure vulnerabilities are identified and effectively addressed:

- **Vulnerability Prioritization:**
  Not all vulnerabilities are equal. It's important to classify vulnerabilities based on their risk level and impact on the system. This way, you can prioritize fixes and address the most critical vulnerabilities first.

- **Fix Planning:**
  After identifying vulnerabilities, it's necessary to plan how and when to address them. Fixes are assigned to relevant development teams, and teams work to resolve them within set timelines.

- **Regulatory Compliance:**
  Organizations often need to comply with industry-specific regulations and standards. It's crucial to ensure that vulnerability management aligns with these regulations to avoid penalties or fines.

- **Continuous Monitoring:**
  Even after fixing vulnerabilities, they need continuous monitoring. This ensures that they do not reoccur or manifest in new ways. Continuous monitoring is an integral part of security practice in DevSecOps.

DevSecOps 3: Application Security

Application security is at the core of DevSecOps. While the benefits of DevOps have revolutionized the world of software development, speeding up releases and automating processes, these advancements have often resulted in security being overlooked. DevSecOps is the answer to this gap, uniting development and operations with security.

Common Application Vulnerabilities:

DevSecOps starts with a deep understanding of common vulnerabilities that can put applications at risk. Developers must be fully aware of potential threats, particularly the most common vulnerabilities identified in the OWASP (*Open*

Web Application Security Project) checklist.
This is a crucial step because awareness of vulnerabilities is
the first step in ensuring that applications are resilient
against known attacks.

The OWASP checklist includes a wide range of
vulnerabilities, including "injections," such as SQL injection
and code injection; authentication and authorization issues;
session management errors; cross-site scripting (XSS)
vulnerabilities; exposure to information leaks, and many
others. Each vulnerability represents a potential entry point
for attackers, and developers must be able to recognize and
address them.

To counter these vulnerabilities, DevSecOps promotes the
adoption of preventive measures from the early stages of
the development cycle. This approach, known as "security
by design," ensures that security is not a late addition but
an integral part of the development process.

Here are some of the key preventive measures that
developers should adopt:

- **Input Data Validation:**
  All data from external sources, such as users, must
  be carefully validated to prevent malicious data
  injections, such as SQL injection.

- **Secure Session Management:**
  Ensuring that session and authentication
  management is resistant to attacks like session theft
  and session fixation.

- **Protection Against XSS:**
  Applying controls to prevent cross-site scripting
  (XSS) attacks that can allow attackers to execute
  client-side code in users' browsers.

- **Validation and Handling of Sensitive Data:**
  Ensuring that sensitive data is handled appropriately
  to prevent information leaks.

- **Continuous Updates:**
  Keeping libraries and frameworks used in the application constantly updated, as vulnerabilities can emerge over time.

- **Code Scanning:**
  Performing static and dynamic code analysis to identify and correct vulnerabilities before they can be exploited.

These preventive measures are essential to ensure that applications are resilient against known attacks.

DevSecOps promotes the concept of "shift-left," pushing security into the early stages of development, so vulnerabilities are identified and addressed not only in the later stages of the process but already in the early design and development phases.

Secure Development Practices:

Within DevSecOps, secure development practices are a fundamental pillar. This involves a series of actions that developers must take to ensure that applications are inherently secure.

Let's have a look at the key components of these practices:

- **Training and Empowerment:**
  Training is a crucial element. Developers need to be trained not only in writing functional code but also in writing secure code. They must be aware of major threats, common vulnerabilities, and security best practices. Furthermore, they should feel empowered to take responsibility for the security of the applications they develop.

- **Management of Credentials and Access Keys:**
  Credentials and access keys are often entry points for attacks. Developers must adopt secure practices

in managing this sensitive information. This includes using key management services (KMS) and regularly rotating credentials.

- **Assessment of Security Implications of Libraries and Frameworks:**
  Many applications use third-party libraries and frameworks. Developers must carefully evaluate the security implications related to these components. It's important to keep track of library versions and apply security patches when necessary. Additionally, adopting static code analysis tools can help identify potential vulnerabilities in the libraries used.

- **Detection and Correction of Vulnerabilities:**
  Developers should be able to identify and address code-level vulnerabilities. Static (SAST) and dynamic (DAST) code analysis are essential tools for identifying vulnerabilities in source code and running applications. Developers must be prepared to address these vulnerabilities promptly.

- **Third-Party Usage Threats:**
  Using third-party libraries and services can open new attack vectors. Developers must consider potential threats related to third-party usage and take preventive measures. For example, it's important to ensure that third-party libraries are appropriately authenticated and signed to prevent the injection of malicious code.

These practices aim to ensure that software products are developed with a "security by design" mentality. This means that security is not a late addition in the process but an integral aspect from the early stages of development.

Source code control

Source code control goes well beyond simply reviewing code for syntax errors. It involves a coordinated series of actions aimed at identifying and correcting security vulnerabilities in the code before they can be exploited by attackers.

Here are some key aspects of source code control:

- **Static and Dynamic Analysis Tools:**
  Static analysis tools (SAST) examine source code to identify potential vulnerabilities, such as known security issues or insecure programming practices. These tools verify code statically, meaning they don't execute it. On the other hand, dynamic analysis tools (DAST) test running applications to identify vulnerabilities in the behavior of the applications themselves. Both techniques are essential to ensure comprehensive coverage.

- **Continuous and Iterative Process:**
  Source code control is not a one-time activity but a continuous and iterative process. It must be integrated into every phase of the development cycle, from code writing to deployment. This means that code is constantly checked, and identified vulnerabilities are addressed and corrected in the context of ongoing work. This "shift-left" approach moves security into the early stages of development, reducing the risk of discovering vulnerabilities only at the end of the process.

- **Detecting Vulnerabilities Before They Become Critical:**
  Constant code control allows for the detection of vulnerabilities while they are still relatively easy to fix. This is crucial because if vulnerabilities are discovered only in advanced stages of development

or after release, corrections can be more complex, costly, and risky. Moreover, it may be too late to prevent a potential breach.

- **Integration into the CI/CD Pipeline:**
  Source code control must be fully integrated into the CI/CD pipeline. This means that every time a pull request is opened or an application is released, the code undergoes a series of automated checks to verify the presence of vulnerabilities. This automation ensures that security is an integral part of the development process.

- **Training and Awareness Programs:**
  Developers must be trained not only in writing secure code but also in the importance of application security. These programs can help identify potential threats and understand how their actions influence application security.

Automation of Application Security Testing

The automation of application security testing is a key element in maintaining high-security standards in an ever-evolving DevSecOps environment.

This proactive approach not only detects and prevents known vulnerabilities but also adapts to new threats, helping to ensure that applications are resilient against both known and unknown attacks.

Here are some advantages:

- **Timeliness in Vulnerability Detection:**
  In the world of application security testing, time is critical. Attackers are constantly looking for vulnerabilities, and timely detection is essential to prevent potential threats. Automation allows for rapid and regular security testing,

enabling the identification of vulnerabilities in code or configurations before attackers can exploit them.

- **Consistency and Reliability:**
  Automation ensures consistency in test execution. When tests are conducted manually, there is room for human errors and subjective interpretations. With automation, the same procedures are consistently and reliably applied, reducing the risk of human errors.

- **Scalability:**
  Automation allows for scalability of security testing based on organizational needs. As applications grow in complexity and the number of releases increases, automation is crucial to ensure that every new code or configuration undergoes rigorous security testing.

- **Regulatory Compliance:**
  In many industries, regulations require regular security testing. Automation simplifies the process of demonstrating compliance with these regulations by providing detailed reports on the security status.

- **Adaptability to Evolving Threats:**
  Security threats change rapidly. New vulnerabilities are discovered regularly, and attackers develop new techniques. Automation of security testing allows for easy updates and adaptation of tests to new threats, ensuring that applications are always ready to fend off emerging challenges.

- **Integration into CI/CD Processes**
  Automation of application security testing seamlessly integrates into Continuous Integration (CI) and

Continuous Deployment (CD) processes.

Here's how it works:

- **Continuous Integration (CI):**
  During the CI process, newly developed code is continuously integrated into the main repository. Automation tools for security testing can be configured to automatically perform security tests with each code integration. If vulnerabilities are detected, they are reported immediately, allowing development teams to address them before the code is further deployed.

- **Continuous Deployment (CD):** In the CD process, applications are deployed into production. Before a release, automation of security testing verifies that the application is secure. If new vulnerabilities emerge or already known ones are identified, the release can be automatically halted, ensuring that no vulnerabilities or threats reach the production environment.

DevSecOps 4: Security of Infrastructure and Orchestration

By integrating security from the outset of every phase of the development and deployment cycle, DevSecOps aims to ensure that applications and infrastructure are resilient to threats and respond effectively to potential attacks.

This approach represents a significant step in the evolution of software engineering, where security is not a late addition but an intrinsic component of the process.

Security of Infrastructure as Code

Security of Infrastructure as Code (IaC) is one of the cornerstones of DevSecOps.

But what does it exactly mean?

- **Definition and Management of Infrastructure through Code:**
  With IaC, infrastructure, including servers, networks, databases, and other resources, is defined and managed through code rather than manual configurations. This means that instead of manually installing and configuring infrastructure components, teams use scripts or declarative definitions to represent the desired state of resources.

- **Transparency and Traceability:**
  Thanks to IaC, infrastructure configuration becomes transparent and traceable. Every change made to resources is logged, allowing for a review of modifications at any time. This traceability is crucial for long-term infrastructure management and security.

- **Automatic Security Testing:**
  A crucial feature of IaC is the ability to run automatic tests to detect vulnerabilities in infrastructure definitions before they can be exploited by potential attacks. These automated tests can verify whether resources are configured securely and consistently.

- **Ensuring Secure Configuration from the Beginning:**
  IaC ensures that infrastructures are set up correctly and securely from the start. This is crucial to prevent vulnerabilities or misconfigurations from becoming operational or security issues. Prevention is a central concept in DevSecOps, and IaC plays a key role in this mission.

- **Integration into DevSecOps Processes:**
  IaC seamlessly integrates into DevSecOps development, security, and operations processes:

  - **Development:** Developers can define the

necessary infrastructure for their applications as part of the source code. This practice, known as "IaC-driven development," enables a consistent and secure definition of resources.

- **Security:**
  Infrastructure security is an integral part of application security. Scanning and testing tools can be integrated into IaC processes to identify and address vulnerabilities promptly.

- **Operations:**
  System administrators can use IaC to automate the provisioning and configuration of resources. This reduces human errors and ensures that resources are configured securely and consistently.

Adopting IaC offers significant long-term benefits: it ensures consistency, transparency, and security of infrastructure, helping to reduce the risk of cybersecurity threats.

Furthermore, IaC simplifies vulnerability resolution, ensuring that resources are configured securely from the outset. It is an essential element of DevSecOps and represents a cornerstone for a resilient and secure infrastructure to protect applications.

Containers and Orchestration

The adoption of containers and orchestration has become a common practice in the context of DevSecOps, as it enables efficient application deployment and management.

However, security in this context is of paramount importance. DevSecOps places significant emphasis on creating secure container images.

- **Secure Container Images:**
  Reducing Vulnerabilities This involves creating images that contain only the components necessary for running the application and are free of known vulnerabilities. This requires a strictly controlled and documented image-building process. Image management should include version control and change control to prevent well-known vulnerabilities from infiltrating an image.

- **Role-Based Access Control (RBAC) and Resource Separation:**
  Limiting Unauthorized Access DevSecOps places specific emphasis on implementing Role-Based Access Control (RBAC) and resource separation in orchestration. This approach is crucial for limiting unauthorized access to system resources. Roles are defined to ensure that only authorized individuals or systems can access specific functionalities or resources. This means that developers can only access parts of the system necessary for their tasks, reducing the risk of unauthorized access. Resource separation is equally important. Resources should be isolated so that a potential compromise in one part of the system does not translate into unauthorized access to the entire system. This requires the implementation of virtualized or controlled environments to ensure resource separation and protection.

- **Continuous Monitoring and Timely Patching:**
Preventing Potential Threats Continuous monitoring
of container activities is a key practice in DevSecOps.
Real-time monitoring of container activities allows for
the rapid detection and response to anomalous
behaviors or potential threats. Monitoring tools can
identify suspicious connections or unauthorized
activities, allowing operators to take immediate
action.

The timely application of security patches and updates is
crucial. Vulnerabilities are constantly discovered, and
patches are released to address them. DevSecOps requires
these patches to be applied as soon as possible to reduce
the exposure window to threats.

Access Control and Authentication

Access Control:

Access control is the process of managing permissions for
users, services, and applications, limiting access only to
what is strictly necessary for their role or function. This
principle is vital to ensure that no one has unauthorized
access to infrastructure resources.

- **Access Policies:**
Access policies define who can access which
resources and in what way. Policies should be based
on the principle of the "principle of least privilege,"
meaning that users only receive privileges they need
to perform their tasks.

- **Role-Based Access Control (RBAC):**
RBAC assigns specific roles to users and then
determines which resources each role can access.
This simplifies access management and reduces the
risk of over grants.

Authentication:

Authentication is the process of verifying the identity of the user or service seeking to access infrastructure resources.

Here are some important considerations:

- **Authentication Factors:**
  Authentication can be based on various factors, such as something you know (password), something you have (hardware token), or something you are (biometric recognition). Using multiple authentication factors, known as Multi-Factor Authentication (MFA), enhances security.

- **Credential Management:**
  Credential management is crucial. Passwords should be strong, regularly changed, and stored securely. Password encryption is a must.

Best Practices:

To ensure adequate access control and authentication in DevSecOps infrastructures, follow these best practices:

- **Implement RBAC:**
  Use RBAC to ensure that users and services only have access to the resources needed for their responsibilities.

- **Implement MFA:**
  Require Multi-Factor Authentication to enhance security.

- **Access Monitoring:**
  Implement access logs and monitoring systems to detect and respond to suspicious activities.

- **Credential Management:**
  Ensure secure credential management, including password encryption and regular key rotation.

- **Education and Awareness:**

Educate and train users on security best practices.

Network and Data Security

In the context of DevSecOps, network and data security is a top priority. Networks should be designed with advanced security mechanisms, such as firewalls and resource isolation, to ensure that only authorized traffic can access applications.

Encrypting data in transit and at rest is a standard practice to protect sensitive information.
Encryption key management and data access should be carefully controlled to prevent potential breaches.

Network Security:

- **Firewalls and Packet Filtering:**
  Firewalls filter incoming and outgoing traffic, preventing unauthorized network access. Packet filtering ensures that only authorized packets reach their destination.

- **Network Segmentation:**
  Segmentation divides the network into isolated zones, limiting the spread of a security breach.

- **Traffic Monitoring:**
  Continuous monitoring of network traffic allows for the detection of suspicious activity or intrusions.

- **Virtual Private Networks (VPN):**
  VPNs encrypt traffic between sites or allow remote users to securely access the network.

- **Patch Management:**
  Keeping network devices up to date with the latest

security patches is essential to reduce vulnerabilities

Data Security:

- **Encryption:**
  Data encryption protects sensitive information during transmission and storage, preventing unauthorized third parties from reading it.

- **Key Management:**
  Data security relies on robust and secure encryption key management.

- **Data Classification:**
  Data classification helps determine which data is sensitive and requires special protection.

- **Data Loss Prevention (DLP):**
  These systems monitor, detect, and prevent unauthorized data loss.

- **Backup and Recovery:**
  Regularly perform data backups and plan recovery procedures in case of incidents.

Best Practices:
To ensure network and data security in a DevSecOps environment, it's important to follow some best practices:

- **Security Policies:**
  Define clear security policies and enforce them throughout the organization.

- **Penetration Testing:**
  Regularly conduct penetration tests to identify vulnerabilities.

- **Awareness and Training:**
  Raise awareness among users about network and data security and provide training.

- **Access Management:**
  Control who has access to which data and networks.

- **Regulatory Compliance:**
  Ensure compliance with laws and regulations related to data protection.

DevSecOps 5: Security Incident Management

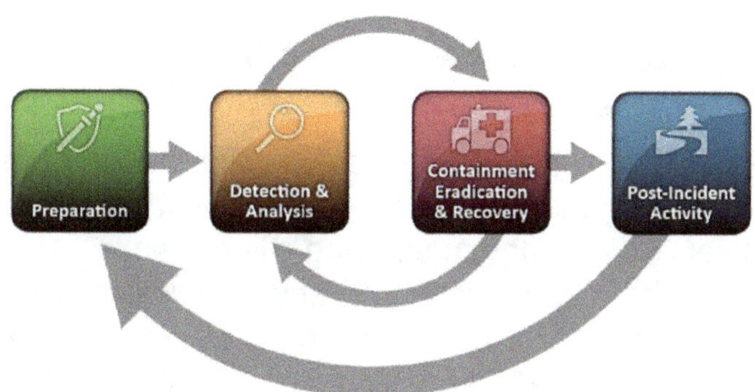

Security incident management doesn't only focus on threat prevention but also on preparation and effective response to incidents.

It integrates security, development, and operations into a continuous cycle of improving infrastructure and application security, contributing to maintaining a safer and more resilient digital environment.

Detection of Security Incidents

The foundation of effective security incident management is the ability to promptly detect suspicious events or security breaches. DevSecOps promotes the implementation of advanced monitoring tools and procedures that allow for the detection of unauthorized or anomalous activities.

Incident detection can be based on signatures, behavior, or a combination of both, with the goal of reducing the time between a breach and its discovery.

- **Advanced Monitoring Tools:**
  DevSecOps encourages the use of advanced

monitoring tools such as Intrusion Detection Systems (IDS) and Security Information and Event Management (SIEM) systems. These tools continuously analyze system activities and network communications to identify suspicious patterns or behaviors. IDS, for example, can detect unauthorized access attempts or cyberattacks.

- **Behavioral Analysis:**
  In addition to signature-based detection, DevSecOps promotes the analysis of user and application behavior. This means monitoring the system's normal behavior and detecting any significant deviations from that behavior. For example, if a user who usually only accesses specific resources starts accessing sensitive data, it could be a sign of a potential security incident.

- **Alert and Response:**
  Once an incident is detected, it's essential to have a well-defined alert and response system. This includes defining standard operating procedures for addressing different incident categories, as well as designating responsible parties for executing these procedures. Furthermore, DevSecOps promotes the automation of incident response activities to expedite threat mitigation.

- **Post-Incident Analysis:**
  After managing an incident, DevSecOps emphasizes the importance of conducting a post-incident analysis. This process aims to fully understand the scope of the incident, identify underlying causes, and plan preventive measures to avoid similar incidents in the future.

- **Continuous Learning:**
  Security incident management in a DevSecOps context is an ongoing learning process. Each incident

represents an opportunity to improve existing security practices and measures. The lessons learned from each incident should be applied to strengthen the overall security of the system.

Incident Planning and Response (CSIRT)

The CSIRT (*Computer Security Incident Response Team*) is the core of the security infrastructure in a DevSecOps approach.

This team is responsible for planning, coordinating, and managing the response to security incidents. Its function is crucial to ensure that an organization can effectively handle security breaches or threats.

Below, we examine key aspects related to the CSIRT:

- **Procedure Planning:**
  Planning is the starting point for managing security incidents. The CSIRT must define detailed procedures that outline how to detect, report, assess, mitigate, and document incidents. These procedures should be communicated to all relevant personnel, and periodic exercises and simulations should be conducted to ensure understanding and readiness.

- **Defined Roles and Responsibilities:**
  The CSIRT must have clearly defined roles and responsibilities. This includes designating a leader and defining the tasks of each team member. This clarity is crucial in emergency situations where time is of the essence.

- **Interdepartmental Collaboration:**
  Incident management is not exclusively a technical task. The team must work closely with technical and

non-technical teams within the organization. For example, it may be necessary to involve the legal team in managing the legal implications of an incident. Internal and external communication is a critical element, especially in high-profile situations.

- **Resource Management:**
  The CSIRT must have the necessary resources to respond effectively to incidents. This may include access to threat detection and mitigation tools, as well as ongoing training to stay up to date with new threats and attack techniques.

- **Rapid and Effective Response:**
  Time is a precious resource in incident management. The team must be capable of responding promptly to emergency situations. This requires clear reporting procedures and an optimized workflow for assessing, containing, and resolving incidents as quickly as possible.

- **Post-Incident Analysis:**
  After managing an incident, the team must conduct a thorough analysis to understand how the incident occurred, which weaknesses were exploited, and how to prevent similar incidents in the future. The lessons learned should be documented and used to improve existing procedures and security measures.

Digital Forensic Analysis

Digital forensic analysis is a critical component of security incident management.

This practice is aimed at thoroughly understanding the causes and effects of an incident, helping organizations enhance their security and prevent future issues. Here's how digital forensic analysis is integrated into the DevSecOps approach:

- **Digital Evidence Collection:**
  Collecting digital evidence is the first step in digital forensic analysis. In the event of an incident, it's essential to preserve relevant digital evidence such as logs, log files, copies of affected data, and any other items that might be useful in understanding the incident. This evidence is collected in a manner suitable for legal purposes and for use in future investigations.

- **Digital Evidence Analysis:**
  Once collected, digital evidence is analyzed in detail. Digital forensic analysts search for clues regarding the causes of the incident, such as intrusions, unauthorized access, or anomalous behaviors. This analysis may involve examining log files, monitoring system activities, searching for traces of malware or cyberattacks, and more.

- **Scope Determination:**
  Digital forensic analysis helps determine the scope of an incident. This involves identifying which data or systems have been compromised, what information has been exposed, and which resources have been involved. This understanding is crucial for deciding what corrective actions are necessary.

- **Root Cause Identification:**
  One of the primary goals of digital forensic analysis is to identify the root cause of the incident. This means discovering how the incident started and which vulnerabilities or weaknesses were exploited by the attackers. Identifying the root cause is essential for taking preventive measures and improving overall security.

- **Preventive Measures and Enhancements:**
  Once the root cause and scope of the incident are understood, the organization can develop preventive

measures to avoid future similar incidents. These enhancements may include implementing security patches, updating security policies, staff training, and optimizing infrastructure and applications.

Post Incident Improvements

One of the most significant features of the DevSecOps approach is its strong emphasis on continuous learning and constant improvement.

After dealing with a security incident, post-incident analysis plays a fundamental role in helping organizations understand what went wrong and how to enhance their security approach.

Here's how post-incident analysis contributes to strengthening resilience and security within DevSecOps:

- **Identification of Weak Points:**
  Post incident analysis begins with identifying weaknesses in the system and security processes that allowed the incident to occur. This might include specific vulnerabilities, ineffective processes, or gaps in staff training. Precisely identifying weak points is essential for taking targeted corrective actions.

- **Assessment of Response Actions:**
  The analysis also examines how the team responded to the incident. This includes the timeliness of action, the effectiveness of mitigation measures, and collaboration between teams. This assessment helps determine what worked and what could have been handled more efficiently.

- **Definition of Corrective Actions:**
  Based on the identification of weak points and the assessment of response actions, targeted corrective actions are defined. These actions are designed to

address the underlying causes of the incident and improve the organization's ability to prevent similar incidents in the future. This might include implementing patches, revising security policies, or intensifying staff training.

- **Process Updates:**
  The analysis often leads to updates in security processes and procedures. These updates aim to prevent future incidents. This might involve redefining incident response procedures, revising security policies, or defining new security metrics.

- **Culture of Continuous Learning:**
  One of the primary objectives of post-incident analysis is to promote a culture of continuous learning within the organization.
  In DevSecOps, it is recognized that incidents can occur despite the best precautions, but this represents an opportunity for improvement. The culture of continuous learning encourages the team to share knowledge, experiences, and lessons learned from every incident.

DevSecOps 6: Compliance and Security Regulations

The DevSecOps approach is built on adhering to security regulations, conducting regular security audits, automating compliance, and security governance.

By integrating these elements into a DevOps environment, DevSecOps helps organizations maintain high standards of security and compliance, reducing the risk of breaches and protecting sensitive data.

Key Security Regulations

Understanding security regulations is essential to ensure that applications and services comply with rigorous standards. Let's delve into some of the key security regulations that impact the DevSecOps world:

GDPR (General Data Protection Regulation):

GDPR is a European law that governs the privacy of personal data.

Its key components include:

- **Rights of Individuals:**
  GDPR grants individuals control over their personal data and requires explicit consent for data collection and processing.

- **Data Protection:**
  Organizations must implement adequate security measures to protect personal data, including notifying breaches within 72 hours.

- **Data Protection Officer (DPO):**
  Many organizations need to appoint a DPO responsible for monitoring GDPR compliance.

HIPAA (Health Insurance Portability and Accountability Act):

HIPAA is a U.S. law that regulates the privacy and security of health information.

- **Patient Privacy:**
  HIPAA safeguards patient health information and mandates stringent security procedures.

- **Electronic Transactions:**
  The use of electronic data in healthcare must be secure and compliant.

ISO 27001:

ISO 27001 is an international standard for information security management.

- **Risk Management:**
  It emphasizes risk identification, assessment, and management through appropriate security measures.

- **Policies and Procedures:**
  Compliance with ISO 27001 requires the definition and implementation of security policies, procedures, and processes.

NIST (National Institute of Standards and Technology) Cybersecurity Framework:

Developed in the United States, the NIST framework provides guidelines for cybersecurity.

- **Identification and Protection:**
  The NIST framework focuses on identifying critical resources and protecting them from threats.

- **Incident Response:**
  It provides procedures for effectively addressing security incidents.

CIS (Center for Internet Security) Controls:

These are a set of critical security controls developed by CIS.

- **Defining Controls:**
  The CIS Controls offer a detailed list of actions to improve infrastructure security.

- **Prioritization:**
  It helps organizations determine which controls are most relevant and prioritized.

Best Practices:

To comply with security regulations in DevSecOps, follow these best practices:

- **Regulatory Knowledge:**
  Fully understand the regulations that apply to your organization.

- **Integration into DevSecOps Pipeline:**
  Incorporate security tests and measures that meet the regulations directly into the DevSecOps pipeline.

- **Documentation:**
  Maintain accurate records of actions taken to comply with the regulations.

- **Ongoing Updates:**
  Regulations change, so staying updated is crucial.

Security and Compliance Audits

Security and compliance audits are procedures used to assess and verify that an organization adheres to established security regulations.

These audits encompass thorough reviews and checks of processes, controls, and security practices to ensure compliance with applicable regulations.

DevSecOps incorporates these audit practices as an integral part of the development and distribution process, enabling timely detection of potential non-compliance.

What is the Importance of Audits?

- **Regulatory Compliance Assessment:**
  Audits verify whether an organization complies with relevant regulations and laws (such as GDPR, HIPAA, ISO 27001, etc.). Compliance is essential to avoid legal sanctions.

- **Vulnerability Identification:**
  Audits reveal security vulnerabilities and gaps, allowing the organization to rectify them before they are exploited by attackers.

- **Continuous Improvement:**
  Audits help identify areas where security practices need improvement, enabling continuous evolution of policies and processes.

Let's examine the key phases of a Security Audit:

- **Audit Planning:**
  - Define the audit's objectives and scope.
  - Identify relevant regulations and policies.
  - Create a detailed audit plan.

- **Data Collection:**
  - Gather documentation, policies, access logs, configuration data, and other relevant information.

- **Evaluation and Testing:**
  - Perform technical tests and assessments to verify compliance and uncover vulnerabilities.
  - Utilize scanning tools and penetration testing.

- **Results Analysis:**
  - Review audit results to identify non-compliance and vulnerabilities.

- **Corrective Action Planning:**
  - Define plans to address identified non-compliance and vulnerabilities.
  - Establish a timeline for implementing corrections.

- **Re-Audit and Verification:**
    - Repeat the audit after implementing corrections to confirm that non-compliance issues have been resolved.

- **Documentation:**
    - Document all results, actions taken, and changes made to policies and processes.

Compliance Automation

One of the challenges faced by organizations in their effort to maintain compliance with security regulations is the complexity and variability of the rules.

DevSecOps leverages automation to streamline compliance management.

Automation tools can be used to continuously monitor systems and enforce security policies, reducing the risk of non-compliance and promoting:

- **Efficiency:**
  They reduce the manual work involved in meeting compliance requirements, saving time and resources.

- **Error Reduction:**
  Automation ensures that configurations are consistent and correct.

- **Continuous Updates:**
  Automation enables the continuous implementation of compliance requirements, ensuring that changes are immediately reflected.

- **Timely Detection:**
  It becomes easier to detect compliance violations in real-time or on a scheduled basis, allowing for a prompt response.

Here is an example of how to automate compliance following DevSecOps practices:

- **Selection of Regulations:**
  Identify the relevant security regulations and standards applicable to the industry and the company.

- **Automation Tools:**
  Use specific compliance automation tools (such as Ansible, Puppet, Terraform) that allow you to define and apply standard configurations.

- **Compliance Templates:**
  Create templates or scripts that define how to implement compliance requirements in terms of configurations, patches, security procedures, etc.

- **Scanning and Assessment:**
  Utilize automated scanning and assessment tools to verify compliance with the defined templates.

- **Deviation Management:**
  Implement processes to handle deviations from standard configurations and define procedures to address them.

- **Notifications and Reporting:**
  Set up automatic notifications and generate periodic reports on compliance fulfillment.

- **Integration into the DevSecOps Pipeline:**
  Incorporate automated compliance checks into the DevSecOps pipeline so that the verifications are executed automatically with each release.

Security Governance

Security governance in DevSecOps refers to the oversight and direction of security activities throughout the organization. This includes defining security policies, procedures, and processes, as well as assigning specific roles and responsibilities.

The benefits that this governance can bring to a company include:

- **Regulatory Compliance:**
  Ensures that an organization complies with relevant security regulations and standards, reducing the risk of legal sanctions.

- **Risk Reduction:**
  Effective governance helps identify and mitigate security risks, ensuring that vulnerabilities are addressed promptly.

- **Strategic Alignment:**
  Aligns security initiatives with business goals, ensuring that security efforts are targeted and efficient.

- **Transparency and Accountability:**
  Defines roles and responsibilities related to security, ensuring transparency and accountability within the organization.

Here are a series of steps to implement it:

- **Definition of Policies and Procedures:**
  Define clear security policies and procedures that outline how to achieve and maintain compliance.

- **Security Committee:**
  Create a security committee with representatives
  from various business functions to define policies
  and governance.

- **Risk Assessment:**
  Regularly conduct risk assessments to identify
  threats and vulnerabilities.

- **Regulatory Compliance:**
  Ensure that the organization is following relevant
  security regulations.

- **Training and Awareness:**
  Provide security training to all staff and raise
  awareness about the importance of security policies.

- **Audits and Checks:**
  Conduct security audits and checks to ensure that
  policies are being followed and vulnerabilities are
  addressed.

- **Incident Response:**
  Define incident response procedures to effectively
  address security breaches.